NO CHARITY IN THE WILDERNESS

Western Literature and Fiction Series

Like the iconic physical landscape and diverse cultures that inspire it, the literature of the American West is imbued with power and beauty. The Western Literature and Fiction Series invites scholarship reflecting on the authors and works that define the creative expression of the past and present while championing the literary fiction that propels us forward.

Genesis, Structure, and Meaning in Gary Snyder's
Mountains and Rivers Without End
Anthony Hunt

The Gambler's Apprentice
H. Lee Barnes

Many Californias: Literature from the Golden State
edited by Gerald W. Haslam

Carol and John Steinbeck: Portrait of a Marriage
Susan Shillinglaw

Sunland: A Novel
Don Waters

Literary Nevada
edited by Cheryll Glotfelty

The Flock
Mary Austin

Exploring Lost Borders: Critical Essays On Mary Austin
edited by Melody Graulich and Elizabeth Klimasmith

The Basket Woman: A Book of Indian Tales
Mary Austin

The Ox-Bow Man: A Biography of Walter Van Tilburg Clark
Jackson J. Benson

The Watchful Gods and Other Stories
Walter Van Tilburg Clark

The Track of The Cat
Walter Van Tilburg Clark

Dust Devils: A Novella
Robert Laxalt

A Lean Year and Other Stories
Robert Laxalt

No Charity in the Wilderness

Poems

SHAUN T. GRIFFIN

UNIVERSITY OF NEVADA PRESS | *Reno & Las Vegas*

University of Nevada Press | Reno, Nevada 89557 USA
www.unpress.nevada.edu
Copyright © 2024 by University of Nevada Press
All rights reserved

Manufactured in the United States of America

FIRST PRINTING

Cover painting: *Border of Stars and Moons* © Shaun T. Griffin

LIBRARY OF CONGRESS CATALOGING-IN-PUBLICATION DATA ON FILE
ISBN 978-1-64779-148-3 (paper)
ISBN 978-1-64779-149-0 (ebook)
LCCN 2023942816

The paper used in this book meets the requirements of American National Standard for
Information Sciences—Permanence of Paper for Printed Library Materials, ANSI/NISO
Z39.48–1992 (R2002).

for my other family—
who must run from skin

But how is this mystery that we humans are?

—Ernesto Cardenal, Cantiga 13, *Cosmic Canticle*

i am, at last, content to leave
the place i've never been
knowing i will never get there

—Wanda Coleman, "For Me When I Am Myself"
Wicked Enchantment

Contents

IN THE WATERLESS WEST

The Moon Outside

Winter Morning, One Year beyond
What Little Democracy We Had

A brilliant sun floods the eastern sky. Again I wake
to light that is not mine and need to know its healing.

Across generations of time it rises to burnish other deserts,
other faces of solace and contempt, the rules of living

no longer with us. The hand I hold in the snowbank remembers
who we are, what dirt we rise from. The poem has no appetite

for saving. We must save ourselves. The certain lines will crest
the day-moon to eclipse my thinking. It is enough to be here.

The redolent wind begins: we are not alone in the time of undoing.

At Mount Rainier

I.

Mountain of memory,
I come to your flanks
in this, the beginning
of my sixth decade, stranger

to the snow, the glacial ice
at my feet, the marmots cold
in their cave of cloud and water.
This is the moon on earth,

the single night of lament,
when I bend from soil,
rise from winter to a pine bough,
a last frozen limb almost free—

this is what I break from,
inhale at eleven thousand feet
and cross, somewhere solemn,
the mountain of many snows.

II.

Then I remember the man
inside the mountain, the cave
of starlight, how he peeled to discomfort,
the foul cry of ecstasy before dawn—

more than water upon its wall of moss,
fern, and impermanent things—
what he left below the canopy
and then, remember, no mountain,

no thing to disturb,
just—

Bringing in the Wood with Cornell

The bees murmur in the Russian sage.
September light slows their wings,
like you after years on the perimeter
of housing in a bushel of razor wire.

We jury-rigged four pallets to stack
two cords of hard and soft wood
in a grid pattern. I said it was a puzzle—
but you are used to that, having nailed

years to the flesh below your back number.
A goldfinch whines in the birch at 6,200 feet.
You become the dust of leaves, ask which
is pine, almond? The weight, I say, and wrest

a limb from its trunk. We jab a narrow path
to the woodpile and sit in the waning light
broken into rounds, quarters, kindling, how
dormant wood dismantles time served.

Your leg is bloodied with the piece I tossed—
a stain of inches, of lying in wait for this day.

Driving My Neighbor to the Pot Dispensary

both of us old enough to remember
when a dime bag was almost enough
for the screech of Vietnam, his beard
to his neck, hair not much farther.

His partner stiff in a wheelchair—
no prosthesis, no channel to the foot.
It was not for ridicule we drove
the snowy road to buy her relief.

Now the war is over money,
how the feckless one will spend it—
on the wall, the weekly coronation?
We drive home in silence, wish for

absolution. A snowflake licks my face
but the storm in her petulant limb
will not subside. He leaves at her door—
neither of us is high nor happy.

Pear Blossoms in the Rain

for Jim McCormick

All afternoon they spoke of you—
and the rain started—the stammer
to rooftops, to tongues who wanted
to praise you, artists, friends,
children from the long branch
of Silver City, Nevada—with your
dome of painterly triangles, and
Jeff whispered, "This one cut deep."

In the morning, the pear blossoms
speckled the ground, rain-soaked
fingers ran to the porch, and
there you were—pressing white petals
to earth, to a wet mountain of clouds
and no one saw this artist swing
from palette to soil, the storm
of tendrils digging into our lives.

Old Wolcott Song

in memoriam, David Budbill

How to say
the losses, they stammer on—nothing
to bundle the hayrick of staying alive.
Every day the ringlets of hope rescind
their meaning and we run behind—
solitary with the one who left.
The marquee of sorrow bequeaths
us to its garden—we are alone in
skepticism, in worry of things unsaid.

This man listened
to jazz with Carruth—two Vermont poets
by a phonograph. In the fore-light of fall,
stalks and leaves burnish the earth—
redolent, waiting—where mouse
and mite resume. The Buddhists
bide time with deceit—let it unravel
to shrines or mountaintops. He was like
this in Wolcott—by the candlelight of words.

Clafoutis

for Baron Wormser and Hayden Carruth

Ten years on and the book
of many tongues arrives
in your hands—like a stone
we cannot know—
except to say Carruth
was a complicated,
dyspeptic poet with a vowel
for northern Vermont starlight,
a riddle of consequence for the blades
of chicory in his garden—

which gave us hope
we would build a stone
of import, and when the blood
came to our doors
there would be Carruthian resolve—
but the vowel for this is love,
to which he gave himself entire,
and only now, in the
harrowing defeat,

can such vision be felt
as knowledge. Hayden never had
the breath of you or I—
his smoke, drink, and
baronic wheeze left him
soothed by no one
save Joe-Anne, Rose Marie, and the Bo.
The few who came calling
were wayfarers, poets
on the road to silence.
And this book about him—
is testimony to an idea;
he is a fiction, an anomaly
of supreme pain and affection,

this man I have sent to your palms
as you fold berries into the daylight
out your circular window.

Unbidden

Mother in the window of no words,

of gray, wet hair
sitting inside the screen glass door,

her caregiver's hand
folded on her shoulder like cloth—

mother in the winter of what she cannot

understand—the shroud of Covid
and we siblings wait the patio of

nasturtiums, lavender, and lilies,
the blue midday light broken

with her voice on the phone—

"I'm tired of being put off—"
her eyes closed to our faces,

the purple rings on her wrist
in this liminal land

and we reach for her outline

like birds who mistake a vision
for an exit and turn to the street

in the winter of what's not said.

Early Morning Kayak, Sea of Cortez

I.

When the sun tendrils
down the back and the oar
rises to split the tension
of salt and water, when the age
of this craft overwhelms
and there is no counting its
widening hull, I think we might
float above this seabed
with the great gray heron
who lifts its needle
at our proximity, but still,
we are no more than mist
in this land of many deserts,
a momentary exaltation
we strum with our worried palms.

II.

Dawn on the Sea of Cortez—
Rickett's dawn, Steinbeck's dawn—
somnolent horizon, from what
great mouth did you rise?
I read of the Sand Mountain
blue butterfly and taste its
insurrection over the sea when
three butterflies pass effortlessly,
hours from shore, like us,
back to back in this vessel,
far from any navigable point—
and yet the compass overhead—
how we paddle without direction,
without so much as wings,
drawn to water, drawn to land.

Sisters on the Ridge

Snow banked four feet high and ice
in the turn to your sister's house.

After forty years, my hands hurt
at the wheel without you, without her

image at the door. I have felt it begin,
a subtle undercurrent, withdrawn

to her shore—a geography
I am wont to know.

I gaze from the vituperative dark
to the plural of mother, daughter, sister.

All afternoon what was said
did not matter, you on the couch

with her shelties, stretched like a loom
and she, poised to receive this subtle

rehearsal. For hours it seemed
the prelude went on and then, a calm.

On the ice road home
the sugar pines bent overhead—

the wind of worry would not say
she or you or why. Trust

the afternoon of sisters
close to a failing mountain sky.

In Fall

for K. and M.

In fall, when the words crawl back
and the wood, hardest to split
among years of worried tension—

I recall a time before this—the lens
of a woman, the lazy Saturday beer,
the long boards of snow and water.

What we left in the marigolds
outside of time. We had no need
of mountains or sky—we were treeless

in arbitration, momentary like the habit
of ease. It was enough to sift labor
from fathers, and we small thieves

hurried the mind of love and work,
but nothing holds in this time—
nothing to quiet what is left behind.

When the Doyens of U Street

for Dale and Marg on their fiftieth

When the doyens of U Street
      whose vertiginous leap
            to wed in the Claremont forest—

when a child rushed off
      to land between them
            like the strings on a guitar—

when what they shouldered
      below the milk and chatter
            of work and faith—

when the dormant lives
      could not forbear the roots
            of love and touch they did—

when a sunrise of misgiving
      burnished the years
            and they stood, willing—

I think no human artifice
      can wedge this trellis of two
            and now, fifty years on—

they intone what started
      but summon more than music—
            like water over stone, they remain.

By a Fire in Ballynhinch Castle

She lies close—the hydrangeas
           folded in rainy abandon,
this fall day in the roadside wet,
           the Celt below this bog, and last night
in the pub of poets and singers
           who luted and tin-whistled
at the Alcock and Brown—

to burn the moisture from
           the wood, from she who
dries beneath a canopy
           of nerine lilies and fuchsia.
On the road home, she picks
           blackberries from the thicket
and licks the sweet wine from her hands.

Letter to Erik on the Eve of Leaving My Job

There are parts of it you will hate—
the days when your teeth wreck
over things they did to incite you—
the steady fraying of belief, the edge

at which you peer and try, in a
husk of laughter, to kill the fear.

But all of this is immaterial
because you have tithed long
in the turmoil of this dance—
how you conscript a person to feel.

This is the storm we work in,
not a weather of clouds and wind,
but a veering toward the horizon
without recognition, which,

in any other field, might be large—
like the howl of a lost mind

that returns to rejoice, and
you isolate the thread of love's
antecedent: somewhere a person
lies waiting to be claimed.

Like a water witch, you reveal
the human below, avow
the blood of their story
when these things are not spoken.

Surely it is a feral peace, and just
as surely, a predation we thwart.

Nothing so simple will suffice,
and so I challenge you: lead as if
there were no shadow—not mine,
not others, but yours and yours alone.

Two for Red Pine Who Found Them Gone

I feel older and poorer when autumn arrives.

—Meng Chiao, 751–814

I.

All day in the weeds and wet earth
I follow Red Pine to the graves
of the ancients—each headstone a mask
of what was left unsaid. Plotted
by rulers and buried by rivers, they
spin through centuries like silk.

What magistrate beckons in the dross
of this century? Outside, the wind eats
the dew and peach blossoms, my hands
swollen from digging. The earth resumes
its innocence. The poets lie and listen.

II.

Yesterday they heard Einstein's prophecy:
the sound of black holes colliding.
Two thousand years ago those physics
funneled to the *Book of Changes*.

The sophist sings, the great ones scatter
the ash road. Party of no king or sorrow,
the poets heave with characters;
the steles slide to the ground.

Kind of Blue at Fairfax and San Vicente

for C. and S.

Almost eighty-four degrees in Los Angeles
and Miles burns the static on the dial.

My youngest waited for her like rain
in this basin, fled the hearthstone

to sit at her feet. No one expects to marry;
they discover Whitman's grassy knoll

and wonder why it took so long.
His bride, an ermine flower from the

LA desert, waits also. No speech from her
sunlit lips. This is the dry land they

saved for, the hills of wooded fame
and for this one moment on a Friday

in November, none of it exists.
Only they, on a ridge in Kenneth

Hahn Park, a breeze of silence
before the crossing over to yes.

The Wilderness of Charity

Down to my last seven days,
only art is left on the walls.
A surreal foment of disbelief,
leaving the castle you made.

Thirty years of advocacy
boxed for the shredder—
names, addresses, tossed to waste,
a terrible abacus of zeroes.

How could they know what
reckless saving lies inside:
the op-eds, legislative campouts,
the temerity of dismantling silence?

In school they taught me to serve;
I now serve the trinity
of dissolution, Heraclitus come
my door. When suffering bends

the columbine—hope's perennial
offshoot—we retain lawyers;
when emptiness breaks the skin,
we no longer hunger.

This dressing of wounds, this
human smolder I raked the earth
to find, and yet found no charity
in the wilderness without us.

Trying to Tell My Mother What I Do

Tell me again, what is it you *do*
                in the disquieting light—

      so I may answer when they ask
            what you make with your hands.

I have nothing to offer her
      but a vow to undo silence. My hands
      cannot hold what I combust.

                    My trade is not born of wood,
            steel, or stone.

When people run
            into the reckless open and

      have nowhere to turn
            except a small door in the office

      I step into the cavity of their eyes
like this, I intimate, and push my finger to her brow.
            This is what I *do*, I run with them

to understand what was said, over and over
      in all these days of learning to be who I am.

Beyond the Border

Instructions for Painting in the Tropics

Break the brush in half—
hold the blunt end still.

Brace the eye for flight—
a gnat may intervene.

How unlike the beauty of home—
the humid winds rain all day.

Then, the miracle of tempest—
go to wave making.

The tide portends interruption—
you will finish in darkness.

Before long, the color has dried—
you are part of the canvas.

Iguana light, hummingbird breath—
you sign the image without a name.

The brush flies from your hand—
you are last to see the storm return.

Walking Out of the Desert

Two crows bristle the roadside,
the trail of belief in the morning-scape:
these cholla etch sanctuary for hands,
feet that spring from the cathedrals
of small towns, of borders turning
in the halogen lights. The shadows
stop, slide, slip into canals, a covey
of quiet voices, how the lens
zeroes to the wet upheaval.
And the eyes rove to other faces
that walk from the river,
to a new land, new *frontera,*
a bite of free until the night sky
coughs them into custody,
and before the hour can wait,
a mouth becomes a moan,
a thickening of saliva,
and the eyes return to the path of birds
dropping to rustle the wind.

They Must Get So Tired of Us

I.

walking around their lives,
the indolent stares, the formal
chaos of living beyond the border,
where a border is little more
than a mustache, a drawing
of two countries sleeping together.

This morning in the *correo,* my wife
needed to wipe her brow. A woman
opened her purse and handed her
three white roses. The colonial visit
to places south becomes a suture
in the hail of truncated speech.

I have no wall, no authority to believe
in rust. I left before Columbus,
but the anchor chain trails behind.
I think of the Allende Bookstore in La Paz—
not Salvador, not Isabel, but the last
modifier in descriptive space: beyond,

as in beyond the venal thirst of nations.
This is home to a child
in the bougainvillea, and the frigate
birds circle overhead, unsure
of the cross floating in the palms.

II.

At the *joyeria,* Noe Segovia
soldered the severed heads
of my glasses for two hundred pesos—
about ten dollars. Perhaps a lens
will drape the wall with carnal vision—
perhaps it will lure a surfeit of lives
to its corrugated skin.

Outside his store, I ride an old
bicycle to the intersection
of lazing gringos in golf carts
and mostly tolerant residents:
without trying we have become
a land of two stories—a gurney
of greed topples mid-street.

III.

At the El Moro Hotel
Americans sit by the pool,
read Kindles. Our neighbor
confides, "I only have four more days,"
like being here is a sentence.
A jewelry salesman, he frequents
flea markets in So Cal—
a silver scorpion crawls his wrist.

In the bar, a retired hospital exec
genuflects to the New World Tequila.
He lost a hundred pounds
after the stroke. He is kind,
a fragrant noun in the idyll
that is Baja California Sur.

IV.

The newspaper erects eight prototypes
of border walls. They look like abstract art
trying to find an audience.
Nothing has a point of view,
I think, unless it ceases to exist.
Mexicans sit by the installation, read ladders.

V.

At coffee this morning,
admonished by the newly retired
to avoid the hungry young man,

I pay the bill. The change
rattles my pocket like a visitor
from the Day of the Dead.

All the way to Misión San Javier,
they chant *hombre con nada*.
Perhaps he will grow food in his pockets,
make a rosary of centavos,
hang it over his head and disappear
like the scent of the accused.

VI.

In the body shop, a woman
straddles a hill in the dust.
She tapes the bumper with news—
the PRI rattles to an election win
and sands the plastic *defensa*—
a bumper with spots like old skin.
She has bent for seven years

since *secondaria*. Each time it
brings her closer to what seems
like rent. Maybe it is food she paints
or a lawn on the dirt floor. At night
a dog soldiers from the patio
of tools. An acetylene torch
sleeps in a shawl of moonlight.

VII.

In a hotel in San Felipe,
first sun through the window
to a *panga* in another dawn—
I fished until my hands hurt.

We cross the perforated steel into
America. The tattooed ICE agent asks
in her best, tendrilled English,
"Are you trying to escape?"
as the drug dog prowls the Subaru.

Hours later, in the Sonoran Desert,
the saguaro signal that we're free
from the helicopters, the burrito
captors, and I wave at the cholla,
the saltbush—perennial shrines

to the sudden eclipse of borders.

The Road to Panajachel

Now that I have come to follow
the road to Panajachel, and the wind
sweeps this street to my salted flesh,
I am nothing more than smoke
from the *tortilleria*, fragrance
of flour, dust, and palm, slapping
from hand to hand in the
indigenous apron of her smile—
brown skin like water in the cave
of Los Tres Tiempos, and the birds
recall daylight before this, before
feet scattered rock, moon, and sun
to break bone upon bone, and belief
ran naked into the street like
a stream of a thousand tears.

Topography of the Soul on a Watery Border: Elegy for the Refugee Camp in Matamoros

What they surrendered to get here—
        the open flame of home

two thousand miles south,
        a country without a name to its

scattered inhabitants,
        a place unlike their first memory

of the humid hands of family,
        where the moon begs

forgiveness in the lakebed
        and the rainforest tells lies

to the chainsaw at its knees.

And now, they live on a river—
        the border between a canopy

of beautiful glass buildings
        and the iron mask of a wall.

They eat over the flame they left,
        wash in a small pan

and leave each day with less,
        an equation of forgetting

to register for asylum
        like a meteor that may scatter,

explode in the new country.
        And the place will be the home

they fled by a watery border
        of some who will not swim its banks.

To Yoshiye from the Outskirts of Manzanar

This weekend, in the rust and labor of twenty-seven years,
I tossed your son's fishing lines—deep sea, fresh water, fly—

and read the transcript of a sentence to Lone Pine:
under Mount Whitney you hid in a dress, an adolescent girl,

your family and future husband caught in a village
of razor wire. You lived on the border of creosote bushes

and garter snakes and now, the swoon of revenge stacks
children in detention again. I held your son's fly reel,

grief-ridden in the spiders of dust, and knew one of us
would float to the other side—where children fish

from porch stoops, witness to this place of ice and
wind eight decades on. I see him there, ephemeral,

in the news of a president who pokes the desert
with dry and eerily white façades where the vans

unload faces in the solitary lounge of America.

Letter to Olga

for Olga Hiczuk

*The Argentina we have no longer has solutions,
the country is beautiful but because of the fault of
corrupt politicians that govern us, we are worse off
every day.*

O.H., 13 August 2021, Buenos Aires

I am not unfamiliar with other women
whose namesake pitted them against
rulers with tiny hands that marionetted
high above the land. And your face,
doña of Russian immigrants, in a
post-Peronesque *paisaje*—what the others

cannot see beneath the crowds agitating
for bread, for rice across the bone of
Patagonia. It may as well be confetti
the puppeteer sends them, those
wrinkles in the sky, as if Borges were here,
this trick of staying poor long enough to survive.

I remember the women in the laundromat—
stacking and folding our clothes for the journey home
and the roses you set upon their stainless table—
the tears of mothers, wives, and students
who shook in disbelief when a small gift
crossed their hands and now—your letter

like a bird in the nocturnal sky and those
women in the solemn quarters of their grief
and you with them, matriarch of Barrio Ricoletta,
post telegrams to friends in the north, dear Olga,
coughing, sending smoke and ash to the Rio Plata,
and your words press down on the woman you left behind.

Carta a Olga

para Olga Hiczuk

Esta Argentina nuestra no tiene más soluciones,
el país es maravilloso pero por culpa de los políticos
corruptos que nos gobiernan, cada día estamos peor.

O.H., 13 Agosto 2021, Buenos Aires

Estoy poco familiar con otras mujeres
cuya tocaya se enfrentó con marionetistas
con manos pequeñitas que controlaban
bien elevado de la tierra. Y su cara,
doña de inmigrantes de Rusia, en un
paisaje pos-Peronista—lo que otros

no pueden ver bajo de las multitudes agitando
por pan, por arroz a través el hueso
de Patagonia. Él puede ser confeti
el titerero les manda, los surcos
en el cielo, como si Borges estuviera aquí, este truco
de quedar pobre suficiente tiempo para sobrevivir.

Recuerdo las mujeres en la lavandería—
apilando y plegando nuestra ropa para el viaje a casa
y las rosas que puso sobre la mesa de acero inoxidable—
las lágrimas de las madres, esposas, y estudiantes
que temblaban con incredulidad cuando un regalito
pasaban a sus manos y ahora, su carta

como un pájaro en el cielo nocturno y esas
mujeres en los cuartos solemnes de su dolor
y usted con ellas, matriarca de Barrio Ricoletta,
manda telegramas a amigos al país de norte,
tosiendo, mandando humo y ceniza al Rio Plata,
y las palabras pesan a quien le dejó atrás.

Reading Baldwin in the After Times

I.

 Fonny floats
in county jail like a cloud,

waiting for a hearing that never comes,
a witness that disappears,
a trial lawyer his family cannot afford.

By the end of the story
I run from clouds as only some can.

Alone with the accused,
this waiting goes on.

For others, not seen,
it is like waiting out a thunderhead.

II.

In the decades since Baldwin
broke with Beale Street,
I think about him—
a gay, Black intellectual stifled by
the façade of New York literature,
steeled in the margins of its cautious acceptance.

A cloud without the morning of calm.

In the prison where I teach
the novel repeats like a bad story,
repeats as consequence for what others
view as tolerable, or not intolerable.

Fonny's still there—
running from the rage.

A pacifist without bail.

III.

In all the time I have taught at the prison

there has never been a right
to read anything.

It is, in the parlance of corrections,
a privilege. And then, I remember

the day the warden filled
four, twenty-yard dumpsters with books
bound for the dump.

It must have seemed alarming,
so much to read—
falling to pigeons, seagulls,
things that swarm the air
of refuge.

Baldwin among them. Baldwin behind.

Elegy for a Librarian in the
Place She Called Home

She was a coyote howling the broken stars from their orbit—
peripatetic, haunted, hunted for being Black in a white town.

For most of the night they came, a pack outside her door
to squeal the notes for a librarian in a white town.

What looked like hope lost on a journey to open books—
this diminutive dancer broke with convention in a white town.

To reel in a desk and chair, literature, and still they squealed—
totems for someone who worked the worry in a white town.

She traveled alone, turned the sage and mountain mahogany
to stand outside the room of consequence in a white town.

Bellowed stories like the coyotes, a dirge of what was lost,
an elegy to the mountain she lived on in a white town.

Now they shed the night and crawl away, ramble the canyon
and send their howling to sun and clouds in a white town.

Their echo remains, a sound she cannot dismiss, woman
who walked in the dark light of this white town.

At last she has arrived, a fluted presence on the February
wind, Episcopal, necessary, and certain in a white town.

Beneath the Laurel of Immigrant Ashes

What began as sorrow can only be shame—
The winnowing of children from their frames

Like they are paper, blown from a field,
A silhouette of something wanted, an

Aura that might have belonged to a
Family, but the wind cannot abide this

Dissection: the crush of children
swallowed in a river of supplication,

What became of the road north:
The coyote, the peso, the cross,

How nothing is concealed from its stare,
This dominion of mercurial *soldados*

Who bequest small towns to the feral
Kingdom, and the children look on

From the distance of black and white
Photos, this noose set upon the color brown.

The Sandinista Moon

Now the sisters of the dominant order
bend the scaffold of secular thought, to pray

And open eyes like moons—these children
who cannot see the violence pass, to pray.

But the two-fisted lord has only room
for hands clasped, on the tiny revolver, to pray,

And makers of Central American routine
slide into the pews, willing to labor, to pray.

What, for an hour, might seem like religion,
comes and goes, in the derelict night, to pray.

And hands gather in the Managua park
like stars beseeching the dark, to pray.

Running from Skin

Veteran's Day

At the border, concertina wire
loops from McAllen to Donna
like earrings on women who string
a river without family, children
who sleep in the headlines
of thieves: these young hands
"steal from our portion" and suddenly
the sun corners a life in disarray—
the back wet, *mojado,* the slur
in a creosote bush, awash in sweat
and dirt and denotations of stops
to here, each rib a calculation of
worry, this island of no nation,
no inhabitant save the sour blanket
of heat and uniforms, how the next
outpost of skin will go wrong.

La Hielera

Limbed by our losses
we stumble on to the next
border of safe and certain
choices, all burden of being
stowed neatly in the ice
below. What the mind begins,
the body cannot know.
And in the blue forest
of regret, some portent
of another will emerge—
no story but the self it seems,
bound to the rope of isolation.

If we touch the fine
cloth of reason, if we dive
down low to listen, some
rubble of definition begins—
how little we are without others—
even as we're told to live
without them, this strain
of solitude and worry.
And rely on lesser things—
a last piece of color
in the brown hills
before winter craters in.

La Hielera is slang for the icebox—the room where immigrants are held at the border.

Twenty Watercolors on the Border

In days I will drive to the neon city to hang art—
twenty watercolors on the border and no ICE agent

will nod in approval. The flanks of the Rio Grande
will be as they have for millennia—with the ropes

of tribes strung from south to north. This is the land
of a Spanish saint's vision—Matamoros—

death to the Moors, but it seems the plentiful
wake of history has offered up new names

and the neon helicopters circle from above—
other moons to swim by. A declaration floats

downriver. Like the words once spoken
in praise of the watery border they disappear

to sediment. There is no bitter end save
cold arms on the muddy banks and they

reach, one by one, to angle a way forward
in the orange blade of light at dawn.

In the Waterless West

But the Moon Will Not Forgive

I.

Lying by the fire, nearly drunk
        with exhaustion, the almond
        disappearing in the cold light,

I thought some part of me
        had been released to that sky,
        a wintering I could not reach

before its name came to my tongue.
        I fell again to the white cold,
        the jazz eddied from the box,

the three-note rest, a clarinet solo,
        and my wife walked in to share
        the blue dawn moving into the room.

II.

On this two-lane the scavengers
        follow me. I cannot outrun
        their shadows. A black wing

beats down—what must I say
        to go on—into the torment
        of the desert? Work almost seems

like a beauty of fire and cold
        as breath weaves in and out
        of the winnowing silence.

Walking the Blood Sky of Vegas

this thirteenth of December,
  days from the shortest day,

when my colleagues shovel paper
  to tell their lives, and the road beneath
   my feet is pocked with desert water—

I remember my friend Steve Liu
  and the Mandarin restaurant on Sahara,
   his wife, Shirley, nudging each dish

to my plate, my sticks silent at the table,
  and I would walk again to find him,
   but the poet is gone, Shirley is gone

to live with her daughter in the ribs of Los Angeles.
  Last month I walked Shelbourne Avenue
   and it held nothing save blue-green stars

swollen to ash, and today it is *Avenida Capovilla*—
  a word so unlike the Spanish of its origins
   I think it too has fled definition. But the oleander

blooms and the Russian olive stakes its crooked neck
  at the road edge—my solemn keepers. It is dusk
   and the street is brittle with two lives—

sun and moon. I wait for them to reclaim this desert
  of people hustled to cars, headlights shrill
   with obligation on the infinite drive home.

Driving into the Rainbow

hard wind, rain in the
creosote bushes—the
long climb into the Sierra,
and my mother, alone
in her room with Ida and Rod,
caretakers whose care
cannot undo the weakened heart,

how she holds her cold,
thin hands to mine
and moves the pale
light in her window,
the brief respite in the
rain, family on her bed,
this small uniform of
grief attends her now—

reticulate,
in the failing hour
as I leave for this highway
into the high desert,
snow at the window, my
wife trying to drive
the icy black—what we
tell ourselves to return:

the fluorescent arc will
follow to the other side.

Black Rock Sonata

When the piano rises from the playa
       to accompany the wind, I hear
              the echo of horse hooves in the

alkaline dust, and rain water broken
       on the teeth of wagon ruts, some
              other time burrowing in: how we listen

without knowledge of its origin,
       this prelude for the bluster down-valley,
              into the moment of exultation,

a sonic presence where nothing competes.

Out of the long traverse, this undulating
       drift of silted shores, up from other pools
              of granite, this earthen bowl of

lamentation, the stones and mollusks who traveled
       this tough skin of migration.
              What the footprints say without

disguise of water, a chorus of alkaline voices,
       a chemistry of waiting for the black
              rock collapsed to sand, close to bone flutes—

the tidal breath of sun and moon, this piano
       in the middle of a whitened plain
              whose sound returns to wind without us.

If There Is a Place for Death

for Greg

Having served seven years before
the cancer came, the tattoos
scrawled up your broken wrist,

no room for the dark survey of
this grubbing art. Drummer who
didn't believe he could be hurt—

you symbolized what the other men
wanted: freedom between the lines.
Hard to chain those words now,

but they envied your particular
ride across the fence, and the notes
home gave mother evidence:

poems were more than dust.
You pleaded with me to send
the journal for her birthday and if

there is a death, I imagine your smirk
at having written "About Me, God,"
and read the words to the rueful end.

Red-headed Woodpecker

for Craig and Dez

Sun was low on the eastern sky—
    a crack in the horizon and the occasional
        wing disturbed the quiet. My friend

stood with the camera on the rock outcropping:
    a red-tailed hawk nested overhead.
        I thought it enough to find a raptor

in the binoculars but my friend waved
    down-canyon: in the cottonwoods
        forked off a broken branch

the gift came into view: the scarlet cap,

the white wings, the raucous *kwrrk*
    sailing from its beak. Blown
        two thousand miles off course

this woodpecker migrated from Mexico
    to the West. Not Kansas, not home
        to provide, but Six Mile Canyon—

runneled with gold tailings and a crick
    of treated water, here in the incomplete West—
        regal as sunlight, perched in a web of wood,

this stopping ground, this canyon of greed
    and grief, how is it you opened your arms
        to a chrysalis of color this April day?

What Belongs

In poetry, appearances, like life,
are full of fear and judgment.

—Mary O'Malley

Yesterday, the warden walked by
to a deferent gatehouse salute.
In the chapel, five of us follow
the precise lilt of Mary O'Malley's

"Beeches." We thought of Frost,
but thought his cold New England
would never close the steel dread
we trip with tongues each Wednesday:

what's wrong is never said.
I looked at Griz, Rabbit, Sabin, and Joe—
adorned with my books—and
asked, to whom do we belong?

On the chapel walls, the mostly
Godless spines of forgiveness—
if only something so quick could
shroud this indifference.

On the way out, the weight pile
magically appears in center-yard.
Now they lift without obstruction:
the warden won't get sued

because a bar drops on a neck.
The feral sweat blooms without him.

After the Election in the Desert
South of Hawthorne

Almost to the iridescent bloom of the Wild Cat Ranch,
a red Chevy out front like a rose in the dust,
and farther still, the snow on Boundary Peak
cuts the horizon from earth. Would you lie with her?
I ask myself, with no answer but the sullen pose of monogamy.

November, postelection, in these few hours of caramel light,
and what of us in this fresco of burnt color, of the woman
in the trailer, hidden like an outpost of affection?

The cold hands of morning reach to still the darkness.
On the road edge, the last moisture frozen before dawn,
staring into the mouth of tomorrow, each mountain,
a light of sage, devil's breath, and salt bush.

Crossing into Esmeralda County, I leave her in the mirror.
The frost remains, but as Patchen asked, is it enough?
A crow answers at Redlich Summit and I descend
into nothingness, somehow reminded of the brown country below.
I will name it for her, burnished daughter of paradise.

Today a senator said all we need is a gun, a horse, and
a plain to ride—whose legs have been parted now?
It's almost make-believe until I understand
the desert is a place where rocks cry and a
woman bleeds in the palm of what is left behind.

Barren Breath of Art

for Theo and Quest

Walking the Silver City path up-canyon
      to bottle shards, mosaics of bed springs and
            TV screens, desert artifacts in an open air

museum, how even the trees of heaven droop
      from lack of moisture, the endless dry that
         is home, but still, the ceremony

winds uphill with plastic flowers, coffee cans,
      and commodes. A tarantula crosses the tailings,
         migrating to Devil's Gate, crawling up

and down until the last turn when the bulldozer
      takes it all away and the road disappears
         into a mine shaft, the coil of art not quite

enough for the greed in its wake, outposts
      in the broken land like some horse of a West
         without plunder, without a gold gone too far.

Twenty-Nine

It is the third day of autumn
and the torment of wind has slowed.

The spider at the window
swallows the lone fly to enter.

Yesterday, I drove six hours in the desert—
a rabbit in the waterless West—

then awoke to your cry:
I will not move without you.

Is there a primrose to guide us
across this land? You ask where

the one river ends, and I point to the white
basin with blue-green light overhead.

How can we hide from its beauty
in this, our twenty-ninth year?

We have nothing but the smoke
of distance to begin this turn of age.

Thinking of William Stafford in the CO Camp, Burning the Dead Limbs Thinned from the Flowering Cherry

For a rose of reasons, the central stem
       breached into sky, the wooden hand
       pulling a southern star to ground

and knew it was dead but went on
       as if to turn the lathe on its
       grain, its cracked skin.

There was nothing but leafless shadow,
       a rhythm of reaching before
       snow and the dark wild

sent it to silence. A calm in the middle
       of an old precursor to death:
       the dry insurrection of tissues—

papery tension, a tapestry of weakness.
       Window to the stiff limbs without
       the tiny parachutes of purple

leaves on the rocks and dirt. Until one
       January day the limbs were cut
       and stacked like serpentine bones

gnarled for flame and the trunk
       fanned out to winter light,
       spare and hesitant. A plume of smoke

circled to wind and another dark
       crept on in the cherried ash
       to a place of starting over.

Leaving the Tonopah Conservation Camp

Seven miles to the white cairn on Highway 376,
and a small, brown woman unlocks
the chain-link fence. Inside, her coworker
double backs after a sixteen-hour shift

in the cranky sundial of corrections.
My friend floats behind the steel door like
a cloud. His arms are bulked with sweet
rolls, popcorn, and Keillor's *Good Poems*.

We talk for two hours, fifteen minutes—
letters, poems, and sons. I read "The Peace
of Wild Things," try to imagine
Wendell Berry in Big Smoky Valley.

If only it were a smoke of ancestors,
of first beauty in this center of the state.
Across from us, a man twice his girl's age
reaches for her breasts. The dormitory

of visiting people as they were. Outside,
the uniformed woman kicks the gate:
"I'm from everywhere in Nevada," as if an
accolade brought her to these chains.

I return to the highway, the blue tail
of sage at my side. Two more years
in this desert and my friend will leave
the guards who guard the grief inside.

Letter to Shame after the ATM Run

... unlike men with money who have places
to put their shame
these men have none

—Jimmy Santiago Baca

There is nothing I can do—
blood has worn its way to your door.
Last night you were a boy
in the coffeehouse, teething
on the next tool to pawn.
But the tables no longer spin,
and you are not free of their wrath.
In every moment, you owe
someone a bite of your life.

I have come to this city of
wind and sex and lights and it has
emptied you to its streets.
You are posted to the rails
of small things—how will I eat,
whom will I tell—before the
shadow cuffs tumble you away.
A blister no one can see. My friend,
the register has closed. You

blink in the feeble light like
a strobe in the dying sun.
Your time in the broken palm
of this day is over. Yesterday,
I wrote ten things on a napkin—
telegrams to the urge to gamble—
and they were swallowed by the wind.
Today, you wake to the iodine
horizon and clean your hands of loss,

but the stain will not leave.

The wind shuffles in the door
to account for things taken,
things borrowed, buttressed by
a timorous man who smiles in shame.
I used to think you could stop.
Now I watch you stumble from
the gilded throat of a casino
to mean little more than dust.

The Long Desert Sky

for Jess

Cloud-light, points
on the horizon
of volcanic rock, sage
and damp earth.

The White Mountains
etch the desert floor,
the gray fingers
running down.

What I believed
in this post-pile land
where I lost
my best friend.

In the smoke of almost
thirty years, I remember
spreading your ashes
on Mammoth's ridge

beneath a lightning
sky like this, and driving
into Bishop from the snow
of Montgomery Pass,

wrinkled now in my aging—
you must laugh,
how we rode down
this highway in your Ford

Econoline Van to ditch
work in our twenties
and years later, cannot budge.
The miles cement a choice—

without the usual banter,
I learn to abandon

this road and lie awake
with your absence.

Nearly to Manzanar,
your family scant ghosts
on the perimeter,
I reckon with the twin selves

of this anguished sky—
another dusk of rain-soaked
meridians through the image
of a man I cannot forget.

Cactus Wren

for Susan

For over a quarter century
    you stowed the seeds of art
        in a wilderness of wrens.

    When there was no money—no
banal excuse, you understood
        its inviolable outline—

a dandelion in the rocks and dust—
    something few were prepared
        to witness: this wild unfolding

    of art in your hands.
Although doubt has driven most
        from the desert, you belong

to the roots of jazz, watercolor,
    flamenco, and the repose of poetry.
        Now they gather for you.

    They learned to live alone
but reach to say goodbye.
        This pantheon of exultation

is blood to your being.
    Like the wren with the gift
        of first light, you scour and surprise.

Soon the Swifts Will Darken the Sky

Over my head they circle
screaming for insects at dawn.
Wings of pepper in the sky.

Before the Morning

Alone in the empty forest, I have
an appointment with white clouds.

—Wang Wei, 702–762

Twenty degrees and the snow eddies
in the window. How do I name

ten thousand flakes? In the autumn
of my sixty-fifth year I have closed

another book and these words
fall to silence too: the brush

of wind exerts a greater weight.
Again, I return to the masters:

Wang Wei atop the blue spruce,
startled from his thousand years

in the forest, recites a poem to the
morning I give away. Snow deepens

to quiet what I once believed,
and Wang Wei stoops from the spine:

this is how you become silence,
how the blue candles reach for

the next generation in spring.
There is no wind to remember

the white breath of this day.

Acknowledgments

The author is grateful to the following publications and galleries where these poems first appeared, some in slightly different form:

"Before the Morning," and "Running from Skin, in *Westchester Review, online* 2020.

"Walking the Blood Sky of Vegas," "Instructions for Painting in the Tropics," and "Early Morning Kayak, Sea of Cortez," in *Meadow,* 2019.

"The Road to Panajachel," in *Shoes,* an art and poetry exhibition at the Sierra Arts Foundation gallery in Reno, 2019.

"They Must Get So Tired of Us," in *Limberlost Review,* 2020.

"Driving into the Rainbow" and "After the Election in the Desert South of Hawthorne," in *Limberlost Review,* 2021.

"What Belongs," in *Margaret, Are You Grieving,* an art and poetry exhibition at the Nevada Humanities Gallery in Las Vegas, 2019.

"At Mount Rainier," in *An Amazing Eclectic Anthology,* 2016.

"But the Moon Will Not Forgive" and "Cactus Wren," in *Ocotillo Review,* 2021.

"In Fall," in *Creosote,* 2021.

"Thinking of William Stafford in the CO Camp, Burning the Dead Limbs Thinned from the Flowering Cherry," in the *Friends of William Stafford Journal/Newsletter,* 2021.

"Beneath the Laurel of Immigrant Ashes," in *Comstock Review* (second prize in their annual contest judged by Juan Felipe Herrera), 2021.

"If There Is a Place for Death," in *Witness* online, 2022.

"Black Rock Sonata," in *Felt Like Five,* a dance and poetry performance by Collateral and Co. at The Virgil, 2021 (poem commissioned for performance).

"La Hielera," in "Border Stories—Looking Beyond the Wall that Separates," in *Double Down,* the Nevada Humanities Blog online, 2021.

"Sisters on the Ridge" in *Limberlost Review,* 2022.

"Red-headed Woodpecker," in *Dawn Songs: A Birdwatcher's Field Guide to the Poetics of Migration,* edited by Jamie K. Reaser and J. Drew Lanham, 2023.

For permission to reprint the following epigraphs:

Mary O'Malley, epigraph to "What Belongs," from an email reprinted with author's permission, 2022; copyright © 2022 by Mary O'Malley.

Jimmy Santiago Baca, from "Tire Shop," reprinted with the author's permission, 2022, copyright © 2022 by Jimmy Santiago Baca.

About the Author

SHAUN T. GRIFFIN has dedicated his life to creating a caring community. He and his wife, Deborah, founded the Community Chest in 1991, a nonprofit organization that directs more than thirty programs for northern Nevada, including hunger relief, service learning, counseling, drug and alcohol counseling, early childhood education, and art and social justice projects. Griffin taught a poetry workshop at the Northern Nevada Correctional Center and published a journal of the men's work, *Razor Wire*. He is the author of numerous books of poetry and prose, including *Because the Light Will Not Forgive Me: Essays from a Poet* and *Anthem for a Burnished Land*. In 2014, Griffin was inducted into the Nevada Writers Hall of Fame.